Stolen Love Behaviou

John Stammers read philosophy at King's College London and is an Associate of King's College. His first collection, *Panoramic Lounge-bar*, was awarded the Forward Prize for Best First Collection 2001, shortlisted for the Whitbread Poetry Award 2001 and selected as a Poetry Book Society Recommendation. He was appointed Judith E. Wilson Fellow at the University of Cambridge in 2002. His pamphlet *Buffalo Bills* was published by Donut Press in 2004. A creative-writing tutor and freelance writer, he lives in Islington, London, where he was born.

Stolen Love Behaviour
John Stammers

Picador

First published 2005 by Picador
an imprint of Pan Macmillan Ltd
Pan Macmillan, 20 New Wharf Road, London N1 9RR
Basingstoke and Oxford
Associated companies throughout the world
www.panmacmillan.com

ISBN 0 330 43386 5

9 8 7 6 5 4 3 2 1

A CIP catalogue record for this book is available from
the British Library.

Typeset by SetSystems Ltd, Saffron Walden, Essex
Printed and bound in Great Britain by
Mackays of Chatham plc, Chatham, Kent

– In my brain's clear retina
I have the stolen love-behaviour.

Rosemary Tonks

to G

Acknowledgements

Acknowledgements are due to the editors of the following publications in which some of these poems first appeared: *Earth has not Any Thing to Shew More Fair*, *Magma*, *Modern Painters*, *New Delta Review*, *The New Republic*, *Poem for the Day* Two.

During the completion of this book the writer was Judith E. Wilson Fellow at the University of Cambridge and Visiting Fellow at Fitzwilliam College, Cambridge. This book was also completed with the aid of a London Arts Board Writers' Bursary and a grant from The Authors' Foundation.

Thanks are once again due to Michael Donaghy, Roddy Lumsden and Don Paterson for their criticism, advice and support. Many thanks to Annie Freud for French consultancy.

Contents

Stolen Love Behaviour

Younger

A hundred lives ago with someone like you
up among the stucco wedding cakes of Campden Hill,
before the absolute estoppel
of split up and the long-range meteorology
of becoming old friends,
before swagger became stagger,
before my first look in the mirror of Dorian Gray,
I stood in front of the big, studio-window
and thought I could really see
the hyper-bright air, the warm days roll in,
the anticyclone isobars
drawn languidly across the southern hemisphere of my life.

Sometimes I see the open window:
in the variegated light that can occur in a room,
in cloud shapes observable after rain,
or when I talk with you of what you will come to do.

Objects in the Rear-View Mirror are
Closer than they Appear

Harrison Ford is driving the huge Dodge pick-up, black and shiny.
The clapboard houses flick past like hoardings with Astroturf verges
as if set there by some wild wag of a realtor.
The setting sun bruises the skyline less and less.
'Some things,' he says, 'you have no choice in – I found *that* out.'
The white line elongates the road.
We are trying to find somewhere to set down,
somewhere to pull the big truck in,
to hunker down for a while.
Everything must settle, she had said,
everything must find its place: her, me, him,
the dust thrown up in the mirror,
the tail-lights heading off in the opposite direction.

Fancy Man

Usually I'm handsome.
I am the well-dressed man who arrives first at dinner parties
and is taking a turn alone around the garden when you arrive.
Lingering at the edge of discussions of social mores,
I express orthogonal opinions over the braised guinea fowl
such as that 'the sex act' is overrated
whereas *conversation* is the most provocative of possible contacts.
My pursuit or occupation is often in the Arts.
Women ask me to talk about my work
and say to their spouses on the way home, 'He's *so* interesting';
they get home faster that way.
Their hubbies fuck them hard that night;
it is uncertain that they like it.
Tell a good joke, slap a good back,
shake a strong hand (the palm slightly turned over theirs).
What's past is most of the things: cocktail bars, ocean liners,
the marginal traffics that call for a nice take on the scope of the lawful.
I have fired a gun,
been threatened at knife-point and felt its tip on my face.
There are cut flowers in my living room.
Sunday afternoons it's the supermarket
for pre-prepared cuisine such as smoked salmon roulade or bruschetta,
full-bodied red wines and the meal-in-a-bag.
My cleaning lady tells me to 'never mind' because 'hope springs!'
Known former girlfriends are young and decorous

and leak sad little tears
when I split up with them 'For *you*, darling, not for me'.
I am still *there* for them
and buy them smart lunches on their birthdays.
Secret loves have been long-time married, had kids.
'He *does* love me,' they tell me.
But that's not love, just a settled form of hate.
They sing out into the air when *we* make love.
In photographs in Sunday magazines
of contemporary buildings and galleries
there is always a room that I am in.
I am there looking out at you in sunglasses.
I stand in the shadows so that you cannot fully see me.
Someone did something to me once
and I have never forgiven everybody.

The Day Flies off Without Me

The planes bound for all points everywhere
etch lines on my office window. From the top floor
London recedes in all directions, and beyond:
the world with its teeming hearts.

I am still, you move, I am a point of reference on a map;
I am at zero meridian as you consume the longitudes.
The pact we made to read our farewells exactly
at two in the afternoon with you in the air
holds me like a heavy winter coat.

Your unopened letter is in my pocket, beating.

Midnight in the Realm of the Psychopomp

This is the Emergency Room, yes, it is New Year's Eve,
it is one minute to midnight in the strange luridity of blips and peeps.
2001 builds like an andante of horn section and timpani,
but there's no Hal or his rapturous flying pretzel of the future,
no voice like the low note of phenobarbitone –
Should auld acquaintance be forgot . . .
The new year will be a space odyssey yet:
no monorail or jet pack,
only the quiet amanuensis of the ectopic beat.
O Hal, calculator of worlds and plotlines,
infinite sub-divider of the space–time continuum,
they have plugged my friend into the National Grid
so that every subsistent thing
is interconnected with him and his bedfellows.
These worldly bodhisattvas,
they are preparing to go, to take their seats
in the featureless cinema of enlightenment.
Fellow beings, do not leave us!
We have need of your quiet counsel,
your implacable lusts and inappropriate hilarities.
The nurses tune into Station X and listen
for the first heartbeat of the new year.
Somewhere a high-pitched beeping goes off;
the room flickers in a green light.

Mary Brunton

Let us walk to the waterfall before lunch
and sail the paper boats we made yesterday;
let us not put away that afternoon of losses
when the August sunshine belted onto the Kerry slate roof
and cooked the lichen to fine sallow dust.
From out of nowhere, I saw you shatter
the blank white page to an angle
and all my flat earth certitudes fell away,
as any waterfall collapses into its pool.
You see, I wanted to believe more than you thought,
but the plain fact of how your fingers
worked the terrible geometries into being
frightened me, the way a child is frightened
by death without knowing why.
This, though, was a coming into the world.
It had not occurred to me to think
you would know how to do such a thing.
You showed me the proper way of it
and so you are changed to me and I to you,
the way that creases remain always
in a sheet of paper that has once been folded.

On Love

Like matters of fact, we worked out the details
of what we would come to call *our situation*.
I said I'd like to see you every week;
you said, yes, you'd like that too.
And, as we stepped out of the *eau de Nil* of the themed *café français*
and into the living consequence
we didn't know we'd brought about,
we vowed, as only co-conspirators can,
that we'd stick to that, not make the mistakes tyros make,
not try to squeeze each other
into the shrinkage cracks in the ageing plasterwork of our lives,
not call *her* by *your* name, *him* by mine,
not fall in love, never that, never that *idée démodée*,
that imbecile, that fool.
Instead, we'd say we liked each other *very much indeed*.

But when I held you to the wrought-iron gates –
my arms large with the weight of our want,
my senses scalded with the direct heat of my own – we fell
into that clearest of all the Februaries:
all pure oxygen and desperate winter sun.

So ensued the curtained afternoons
giving flesh to our one conversation,
and the stark-naked hours of phone calls stretched to breaking point

across the mute city between us
and the director's cuts of the lives we'd never led,
unreleased and maiden from the archives.

Because we'd soon given the lie to the once-a-week fiasco,
our tight flowerhead forced to early bud,
so that twice and thrice and Saturdays and more and more
we tore into one another, hell bent for the heart
of what we gave ourselves and were given up to in our turn.
And what we uncovered was all our love
opened up like a beautiful cunt before us.

Such was our fate, our Next Big Thing, our kismet,
the free-flowing course of events
like a glass of water you can't run back into the tap.
Which is why we turned deaf eyes to the watching audience to come,
because we were over the side by then and could do nothing but swim,
swim our one go in the Nile's water, its Levantine aromas,
that continues at once to drain *and* overflow, louche and inchoate,
taking us up with it as it goes.

La Siesta

Juan Gil-Albert

When I arrive at that secret confine
and they question me, 'What is the Earth?'
I should say a cold place where the dictator overbears
and the oppressed cry long tears
and where, in shadows and gold teeth,
injustice does the rounds
taking up his profits from the men of property
and mankind's permanent tragedy; it is a wasteland.
But again, I should have to say,
when in clear altering situations
the land exhales the somnolence
of not knowing the source of one's fatigue,
while the blue sky pulses like a hallucination
and fruit follows fruit on the white tables
and great windows, set ajar, cool
in the semi-light, we seek out a bower
where we may fall beneath that soft weight.
It is then I should tell them that the Earth
is an original happiness, an inward impulse,
like an unprecedented temptation,
composed of both ardour and renunciation,
a giving up and a giving in, a slow love-potion.

Read

I found you out when you knew all the words from *Blood on the Tracks* by heart. You must have picked them up while we'd driven along. I'd fixed a makeup mirror on the dashboard so you could lip-read as I drove then realised I could play up loud the songs you'd never hear and still mime conversation to you. We would take the old A roads north, stifled in a tedious, Midlands sun, or watch a cloudburst lash the road ahead. We got to be regulars in the lorry drivers' cafés where we could sit face to face across the sauce bottles and Italian formicas. The men would nod a smile across at your atonal consonants and vowels, any such small familiarities being welcome away from home. For once we were part of something: the strung-out, bleary community of the road. And I used to say, 'You make me feel like who I am,' the way you could always tell what I was thinking. But you'd simply learned to read off my mouth those minute flexings and pursings that break through like radio-static from thought. Listen, I never wanted it to be like this; *You – Can't – Treat – A – Lov – er – That – Way.* I catch myself muttering in the street now and then, as I've come to notice old or disturbed people do. But you and I haven't spoken for (how many?) years and there's no one to read the nightmares I mumble into the small hours and all you can hear.

I Don't 'Go Organic' Often, but When I Do

I don't 'go organic' often, but when I do
cash registers explode, shop assistants lurch back
beneath furry earflaps,
   the wild beasts knitted on Iroquois sweaters
          leap up,
their hunters let fall their bows,
  returning, at all fleet, to tented encampments of their tribe
to sit wordlessly
  with the Great Spirit.
     Cram up my basket, I say, for I am not all water –
though hydration may form the signal part
  of any halfway harmonious regime.
I am told that amaranth binds a higher protein content
than the equivalent weight
  of any goodly made walrus.
Pass me that cantaloupe, farmed in biotic growing methods
by organo-wonks with expensive recreational habits.
           I wish to pay
largely for it, if you would be so kind,
  and desire
little change from a high-denomination banknote.
    Only stay, stay your hand there on its surface
to let my own against the edge of yours, tender, as in a slow wooing.
Fresh we were and wild,
     O yes wild, I say, were we,

implacable huntress of the free-range legume.
And what does it come to in any sort of natural currency? –
    a single meal for two, free of human taint,
the feel of cool green skin beneath your palm touched along mine;
and a further difficulty – I see that, scourge of the brassicas –
    I do not always know what I am doing.

Russian Tea

An awning merely obscures the inner café
from incontinent oglers into others' lives.
They may still observe the scarlet tablecloth's affray
of sugar bowl, side plates, butter knives,
or the hot, imperious sheen of the samovar,
its steam tinctured with tannin from the mash,
or, if you will, a couple from Almodóvar.
He leans across – a bone-china clash
as he's led on by the green chutzpah
of her riding coat, the desire
of blood-red soup, painted doll and balalaika
(his spun chamber, his cocked hammer).
She fixes him with a stare,
lifts her cup, takes a sip, pulls the trigger.

Furthermore the Avenue

Furthermore the avenue recedes,
all the tables set out for *le déjeuner*,
tiny crabs are spots of cochineal on saffron rice,
their one pink day is going well so far.
Platters of sea bass, gambas and trinkling glass
do nothing but vie with the C-sharp of Lambrettas
that dopple off down the street to G.

Your features etch an outline in the noon UV,
your profile against the duck-egg-blue sun blind – such a line!
Would you like more of the *salade d'epinards* we ordered? –
espèce de folie! espèce de grandeur de salade! –
less is off the menu.
Vague clouds run their hands through their coiffure,
bring their lips together in a moue.

A look from you on this *cours provençale*,
a smile from you in this air – itself warmed with aromatic herbs –
a word from you could introduce a certain *à propos*
across the reticent white tablecloth.

The day turns, a turn of your head
and a glance along the avenue.

ΧΕΜΑΣ

Centre for Mathematical Sciences, Cambridge

And you are right,
        the ordinals dominate,
which may be interpreted as pseudo-science
whilst in the New Terminologies
        this transmutes to merely *recalcitrant*.

It is as if there is nowhere you have been.
It is as if there is nowhere you have been
'item coherent'
        (that is to say, coherence
in Tarkheusen's sense of hyper entities).

Is there a problematic, subsequent?

Even so. They perform experiments with the clocks,
seek to devise one intricate q-operation
as the basis for all further conjectures
or unplanned behaviours *tout court*.

Will they succeed?

They are early here. No one,
not the least among them,
factual or declined, is numerically 'real'.

I, meanwhile, proceed via computations
which describe complex halfway states
only hitherto suggested by Kusama in certain asequences.

Moreover, I have never been here,
repeat, I have been here.

The Sun Like a Young Visitor

The sun like a young visitor from abroad
has had its last fling. The thrill
of our damp air that banks off the ocean
warms me as much as heat;
I was born to be cold in a chill place.

All you saw of me, all you never saw of me;
the love I hold for you – there are many forms of love –
is absorbed into me and enlarges me.

As you pick up your life, far from our small togetherness,
be more than you were before.
I am sustained by you
as I give myself up to winter's dark mouth.

Closure

'You never really know why you've made the mistakes you've made until you've lived through all their consequences.'

Daniel in *La Porte Grise Ouverte* (dir. de-Vette, 1968)

5.10 p.m.

She pours down the phone at me, sobs,
'John, what's going on? *John!*'
'I'm in a callbox,' I say, 'I locked myself out –
yes, *locked*, yes, *out.*'

11.00 a.m.

I describe a parabola with the ball of my left foot
on his living-room carpet.
I've been caught in the company of uncool friends:
the clinging tracksuit bottoms,
the companionable tea-stained jumper,
trainers like lolling dogs' tongues.
'Taking out the rubbish,' I say.
'I can see it now: the tug, the slam.
It pulled the doormat right out from under me.
And you know that place is like a sealed box
I don't think Houdini could get himself into.

But she's bound to be back sooner or later.'
He says, 'We'll go to the movies.'

9.20 a.m.

I am holding my parents, they are split
in two separate photographs in a box frame.
They each sit in a wicker basket seat at Kenwood
with their easy fifties smiles.
They have taken turns in that same seat
for these Box Brownie snaps,
but I have placed them side by side
after all that elapsing.
A couple of adulterers in the making,
they grin back at the camera.
If they could see beyond it,
past the temporary trees of a particular July day,
if their eyes could focus past the sunshine that strikes them
precisely at the speed of light,
see through all that hocus-pocus,
they would see that they are looking straight at me,
for once not trying to shake off the feeling
that they are beautiful fools,
wedded to the course of events

that flicks up images which appear static
because caught between blinks.
I mouth a habitual prayer to understand.
      They peer back,
turn to one another, he speaks:

'Look at him, always so quick to jump to delusions.'
'What about the tears and rages,
the torn-up love notes, the early deaths?'
'Our lives killed us, everyone's do – he should be careful.'
'Tell him that.'
'Just shut the bedroom door, boy, and enjoy the day.
Look at us . . . and we've been dead these twenty years.'

They turn back to that Eden of gardens,
the fixative seeping away over the years.
I clatter the contents of my pockets from the bedside
and replace it with their photos.

2.15 p.m.

We go see the new Tarantino with its addiction
to jump-cut technique: time sliced up
as if it were nothing so much as a backdrop,

23

a prop to be wheeled on whenever,
time, like a worn-out old actor from the forties
who once slept with Rita Hayworth,
but who is now just grateful for a cameo as a gutter drunk.
'Who's Rita Hayworth?' asks the key grip.

9.15 a.m.

I run my hands over and over my poems,
lay them all out on the bed.
I am given up to these secret lyrics.
Through them I enter that reversed zone
between the silver and the mirror
where the clock runs backwards to time
and I act out absurdist soliloquies of lost love.
I think I can keep it all separate, hold it all apart,
keep it in me, in the poetry. In the living room,
Otis Redding's alive and intoning;
the mortal timbre of his voice takes its toll.
I glance across at my parents smiling out into the light,
go over and clasp them in my hands.

8.45 a.m.

The kitchen reeks of stale compromise
and unpalatable accommodations. She eggs
me on to cross knives with her. I don't.
If I could work up the appetite
we wouldn't be here,
facing into the face of each other,
in the first place.
        You can hear the hiss
of our brand new Russell Hobbs;
the chords ascend sibilantly: the fourth, the fifth.

        In the name of all that's nameless,
she accuses me of an affair.
She doesn't know the reason I never could
isn't because I don't feel that cold nausea for it,
the grope at breath that at some party
my mouth is going to say 'I was just wondering . . .'
and I'm *married*. No, none of it –
my parents, they made me this way.

        I catch myself in the kettle's chrome:
a tiny bulbous shape puzzling at itself.
The steam rises like ectoplasm;
something is leaving its earthly form.
        I hold my breath

in this locked, chained and buckled box
submerged in six foot of dirty dishwater;
my lungs are shot and I'm gagging.
I should clarify: my body remains stuck fast
to the seat-vinyl of the kitchen chair,
but someone in me, someone I'd forgotten I even knew,
decides to make a clean break for it, to take charge and say:
this is it, we're leaving, no more of this shit,
nothing, nil, nought, nix;
say goodbye to Manderley;
Grab your coat and get your hat . . .
It's then I hear my own voice saying:
'Let's just give it a little more time . . .'
Exit wife from flat, at this point.

2.35 p.m.

My friend sits with a silo of popcorn on his knee –
he's from America; they do things differently there –
he erupts in white froth at the film.
It's as if there's not enough effervescence on the screen.
Perhaps it excites some awful froth need in him
as we watch Travolta resurrect himself
with automatic handguns and heroin,

26

see the horrible ifs accumulate, the stiffs agglomerate,
the action roll itself backwards
to where Pumpkin and Honey Bunny get let off with their lives,
the one place in the film that will do for a happy ending.
As if that would be, or as if there's something awry
with unhappy endings, things finished,
something completing its rightful term,
coming down to no more than a memory,
some love songs and a couple of old photographs.

5.15 p.m.

Back in the phone-booth and she's still screaming,
still screaming about 'these poems',
'these poems about this woman, this (she says *her* name).
Who is she, John? What's going on?'
In a few frames the day folds up around me
like a cheap car in a crash,
concertinas bit by bit in slow-mo,
a scrunching French kiss; it all rushes at me:
the photoframe, the popcorn, the poems.
'I'll come straight home,' I say. 'I'll explain.'
But I don't want to explain:
it's all there on the bed.

10.13 a.m.

It's that morning and I'm outside the flat;
the bin bags are there in front of me,
as are John Travolta and the misplaced keys,
the poetry, the phone box and the end,
when I turn, with nothing in my head
but the dead vowels of Otis Redding,
lost love and getting shot of the rubbish,
stretch out my arm for the front door and see it closing.

Nom de Guerre

The heatwave has brought forth all manner of blossom:
there are alcoholics in the gardens
of the church where my parents were married.
In the late afternoons, they lambast each other
with what life and death scenarios of the day.
They have special names like *Dogsy* and *The Surgeon*.
If I ever park myself back on that particular bench,
I'd like a special name.
I wish my life were more coherent.
The pavements are sweating a sort of grey gunge.
I have lost the ability to imagine winter.

Between a Rock and a Hudson

He steps out of the standard lamp's narrow stardom
into the shade that dare not speak its name.
Brylcreem and the immaculate swank
of pink-piped pyjamas and silk *His* bathrobe
set off linebacker shoulders.

Doris sings in the shower,
sings high in the plashy ecstasy of wet hand and sud:
Que sera, sera . . .
She has peeled off Day for the day and left her
a crumpled body stocking of apple pie on the tiles.
She is doing her own thing for once,
singing a wet tease for the habitual scopophiliac of the lens.
The zoom drive whirrs itself to a close-up:
the soap-down of the girl next door
who has forgotten to pull the blinds
just for fun.
        From out the left
Hitchcock is casting himself
against type onto the shower curtain –
everything has had bubbles in it so far, after all.

Botticelli might have styled her as reaching out
for the long blue slab of the soap,
made to catch her rise or bend to cup her breasts

beneath the lick of the water's multitudinous tongues.
Rock's away with the *Forty-Niners*,
the pectorals gleaming like trophies from ancient Greece.
While inside the flickering peepshow of 35mm,
Doris is bathing mid-frame,
caught on the half-shell of the shower tray singing
whatever will be, will be . . .
married, cinematographically, to a man who wants a man,
filmed by the outline of a cameo,
the future's not ours to see . . .
watched by us. Cut!

Exotic Scents

Charles Baudelaire

My eyes shut in the closing light,
I inhale the aroma that rises from your bosom's heat
and see extended a fortunate shore
dazzled beneath a flat sun:
a lackadaisical archipelago
where are peculiar trees and fruiting plants,
men with bodies lithe and smooth,
women who shame you with their look.
I am led by the perfume of you to these indolent climes,
to a lagoon where sail and mast nod
in the dead fatigue of the ocean's demand and pull.
That's when the scent of green tamarinds
modifies the air, inflames my senses,
couples in my soul with the songs of the deep-sea mariners.

Rive Gauche

after Charles Baudelaire

Lids clamped in the black-eyed longueurs of Sunday's p.m.,
I detect a retrograde odour giving off your skin;
last night in the *Archipelago* flashes back again
like the stab of lights at the onset of a migraine:
the south sea island, basement-bar disco –
its coconut-lush, its static palm fronds,
hunks like torsos in a menswear shop window,
tottie who lovebite from their assorted backs of beyond.

It's *eau de cologne* that leads me by the nose to this outpost
of glam where barstaff and bouncers blear
into the welter of the night's pulls: the excess
of *ad hoc* endearments and faggy snogs. See how *Rive Gauche*
overlays the mouldering aroma of damp here,
colludes in your bed with the smell of our sex.

Mother's Day

Beneath a fractured intercourse of shadow
and streetlamp, two people are foregrounded, black on white.
They are trying to say goodnight
to each other without success. As he pulls to go,
she pulls him back to her; as she retreats he advances,
catches her up again.
        They have been here half an hour
in the last phase of the leave-taking they go in for:
hands at lips, bit-off votives in the throat and back glances –

all essentials in their breathy rhetoric of parting.
Him: 'Past their bedtime?' Her: 'A suburbanite
turns for home?'
        They have stopped the night,
the two of them, who are now trying,
with no goodbye, to make no tomorrow.

He says, 'Go . . . No, stay! You *must* go!'

John Keats Walks Home Following a Night Spent Reading Homer with Cowden Clarke

Brother, your comely hypotheses trouble
the quiet waters of dawn streets; as mercury
integrates to a constant self-fascination,
so a puddle's surface would retain the home-bent form:
here passed one whose shape was graven in rainwater.

Your rough coat gripped round you on that solitary march,
your attention is elsewhere to the moment while you travel
not by Cripplegate or Leadenhall but Troy:
the thousand walled narratives of a city slumbering and silent
before day and the dead clap of bronze on bronze,

the flat plain of Finsbury Pavement fell away to sand,
and Patroclus come to a young death on Mars' field. Apothecary,
you let the fevered blood of your imaginings into verse.
These are visions, visions born to survive, as you beetle
beneath the fixed planets across London Bridge.

God blind me, the star-struck heavens you contemplate
contemplate you in their turn, singular beacon
whose unrepeatable illumination inspires
ordinary readers at this particular remove,
so countenance that innocent vanity

which claims an association to a special realm.
Now at your desk, you lift your pen,
mutter something lost and begin to write.
Daylight finds you trophied in ink, clouded in near-sleep.
By first post, you will be a masterpiece.

There

I survey the scatter of your flat, the origami paper ball
pendulous beneath the chandelier.
Giant sequins that are face-down CDs
reflect some acute angle of incidence
of the lightbulb's lugubrious, moody loll,
their leitmotifs rippling the light in grooves:
Lieder, Liebestraum, Love me Tender.
It's like one moment you are not there
and then you are,
as if an assistant has activated an arc lamp for a photo shoot –
whoosh!, woman of weirdy shapes around the house.
Your sculptures are unique forms of sounds in space,
the silhouette of your sobriquets, say:
Rachel, Raquel, Rach', Rachem.
You are as intensely real this instant as an image
on the front cover of *The Face.*
But who? I don't know you girlie, girl.
Then Rachel everywhere,
Rach', all around in your actual front room –
tint and timbre and oblique, spatial trajectories! –
so that I can see you, really see you, Rach'.

Rosegarden

There's bound to be rain after all this. The unholy heavens
are black bouquets laid out along a mantelpiece.
Interrupted from being who we are for a moment,
we turn and look through the big bay-window
to the rosegarden and the red, red roses.

And I go to say the same thing as always:
the way the folded intimacies of their flesh
can take me back to any weekday afternoon
when we were in full bloom, when the perfume of us two
would open up into the room.
                                                    Instead I hover
like the gadflies in their airy-fairy concatenations
caught between the lily and the rose.

Remember the story of how the rose got its red? –
how it spiked the Sultan's daughter
when she took it to her face to take in its sweet breath,
her lifeblood spilt from her whitening body as she stumbled
into the pale spirit she was about to become.

The defunct telephone is hollow as a bowl;
the vacant stilettos are on the bedroom floor;
the blunt daylight murders the thought
you could be standing there in a dark corner, standing there

waiting for one last charming lark,
the idea we could ever be anything
other than someone we once knew
in horticulture.
                    The princess' lover, it's said,
laid a single stem on the white expanse of her sepulchre,
the soft petals drying to nothing over the brief days and weeks.
I could hang around like a delinquent rose
desiccating slowly in the elements.
Then you incline and hold your gaze in the mirror
as if you can see straight into the mind of God,
'Coming back would be like some turning away.'

The first drops of rain detonate on the flagstones.
I beg your pardon, go outside to see the roses.
Look, don't they remind you of something?

The Other Dozier

Holland Dozier Holland

Two Hollands and one Dozier. But I have here
a faded promo bill that names a second Dozier:
Lamont's cousin Montal. He's the one
who had nowhere to run to, nowhere to hide
his systemic abreaction to soft gospel and pop discography,
who couldn't get a witness at any price, just couldn't take
the break of Soul or the ache of Tamla to that old heart of his,
like the one gun-shy Earp or the only Flying Wallenda
with vertigo. Turns out he had a tin ear
for everything except irony,
so his lyrics all emerged as modern verse:
reworked tales of Bathsheba in a cool style that exploded
to no one, a murky, uncharted Petrarch,
while his cuz and his two best buds cruised the Detroit streets
inside a petrol-blue stretch limousine
glazed with rain.
                          So much depends
on which ending you favour, which of the many
that may or may not have befallen this extra man
whose name was written in square brackets.
There's an old guy with a corner tobacco shop
who plays nothing but Rachmaninov and Mahler,
who'll tell you, if asked, yes, he does know
what the word *Tamla* actually means
and who the fifth Top was, or that he had a poem,

one time, published in the *Midwest Express*.
Of an autumn night he sits on a small balcony
high above the motor city –
the urban inversion, the gasoline wall of sound –
writing poems of loss to a Vandella.

Selected Sentences and Sub-Clauses from
Early Chapters of *Wuthering Heights*

Hareton Earnshaw was performing his orisons *sotto voce*.
I let him enjoy the luxury unannoyed.
There was such anguish in the gush,
bestowing himself in the vacancy.
The females were astir,
Zillah urging flakes. Just finishing
a stormy scene, poor Zillah,
employing an epithet as harmless as 'duck'.
Having no desire to be entertained by a cat,
my landlord hallooed for me to stop.
My human fixture and her satellites conjectured.
I dragged upstairs to restore the animal heat.
What vain weather-cocks we are!
I desired Mrs Dean.
Hareton Earnshaw has been cast out
like an unfledged dunnock.

Two Japanese Girls at Bank Station

Two Japanese girls at Bank Station provide an instance
    of ultra-black with their hair, their acidity
all expressed in the citrus colours of their clothes.
      Perhaps they are waitresses
in a sushi bar in the city
    – there are more of those now, so many –
and they change in the back room into total black
so they are transformed into characters in a Noh play:
black-on-black
        with chalk-white faces
as they totter the tables
        presenting dishes and dishes.
Their strange magazines with the perpendicular text of characters
        and their bright, bright colour pics
captivate my eye, to blink is impossible, are they 3D?
    That would be mesmeric, as all *Japonaiserie*.
This is the Japan of movie time,
    of the blue-deep-blue business suit and bushido,
where a man may be discomfited by the sideways look
      of the karaoke bar hostess,
or eat raw fish at a street kitchen under hard rain;
this is Fuji-color in a Nikon camera
to photograph a thousand wet faces,
      like petals, on a subway train.

Akirana, take me
to the Japan of the graphic animation process,
        Japan of lucid dreams,
Japan of neon-neon light and Coca-Cola.

Dead Trees Shed no Leaves

Under the parklife's baffled surveillance,
before the plane trees threw off their hands in resignation,
we sat in the deserted car park like double agents
exchanging sensitive items of information.

Empty trees attempt the flake-white sky,
yet fallen branches hold to their dead leaves, tragically.
We played us off against each other, those two,
you telling me to me, me telling you to you.

It's a Wise Goat that Knows its own Foodstuffs

I am forced to explore grey
which is, after all, as true as vermilion
or cobalt blue and more pervasive actually,
being the colour of the surface blur as it is. We all know,
don't we, that you should become longer sighted
the older you get. It's just that
you have to have biblical longevity
for it to make a difference. They don't tell you that
in the local anecdotary and I must say
having to do without edges is a blow;
who'd have thought melding would have its day!
O give me a home that doesn't look like amorphous foam,
I feel like singing at my desk, but decorum forbids.
And would it be worth it? Naturally.
It's just that a snooze in the afternoon
has it over white-water rafting, Bayreuth,
or even betrayal (that slickern jackal).
A sandwich for convenience, a duvet ditto,
a long-wave transmission on the radio,
and don't mention sexual congress or thighs –
I have known them both and found myself wanting.
And when all is said and done
there'll be nothing more to say or do.
Which is an odd thought,
like looking forward to St Bartolph's Day, or nettle soup.

Three Chüeh-Chü

after Tu Mu (803–852)

On the Road

In recurrent Main Street family diners, I dine alone;
these food stains are permanent on my *Valentino*.
In local bars I drink the health of the one poet there,
teach a soft girl to blow old tunes on a trombone.

Recalling Former Travels

Trapped in a flash flood twenty miles north of Danvers;
snowbound in the elbow of the big Columbia River;
heading west by night so as to stay unnoticed;
the ringing in the wires, the country songs of the truck drivers.

Easing the Heart

In the places that are behind places, I ranged, self against self;
Angelica's svelte frame tore my heart, her complexion like Delft.
Ten years on, I awake from an erotic reverie by Schiele
to the name they give me in the red-light districts: *He who drifts.*

Green

We bit the green blood, we bit the bitter leaf,
sweet, of the mahonia tree.
You held us up the broken twig, the taken sprig,
the smell of its petals helter-skelter in the air.
And I took it in my teeth as if it were your nipple
when you offer it to me, the nip
of my incisors' serrated edge
on your flushed and more flushed areola.
You bit, and I too, the tree's green life-blood,
the flowers, all around, the yellow derangement.
Later we looked up poisonous trees.

Prairie Rose

Inside my dream the towns fall by us one by one:
Laredo, Rocky Neck and Sprute.
I am asleep beneath the jury-rigged tarpaulin
in the night cot of your cousin's mobile home,
the air thick as corn soup.

The tyre noise slackens as we pull in at
a drowsy joint called *Maria Eleana*'s.
Her jukebox sings dobro and Hank
and an outfit called The Tuscaloosa Boys.
The intricate needlework on your boots
twinkles like pinpricks in black card
and the liquefaction
of your denim bolero
as it sidles to a bluegrass waltz
hits me over the heart like a high-calibre round.

'Wake up, wake up,' you shook me,
'there's a tornado headed this way.'
And I saw that Satan's index finger
doodle devastation along the highway.
'Kansas this ain't, Rose,' I explained,
'and there's no way home.'
'But we *are* home.'

The Truth in a Position

for PI

The macramé plant hanger dangled in the Santana airflow
the last time you and me shared a gas,
the last time we slapped each other's backs
and let out a cackle at some facile bit of sarcasm
we colluded in styling as satire –
high fucking satire, at that.
El Condor Pasa's flethered nose (or whatever it was) flute
was blowing down the breezy avenues
of the well-heeled inner burbs
whose parties we got ourselves into
as mates-of, or mates-of-mates-of, or just plain curiosities
with how we could converse against type
like *idiot savants*.
               I recall how, to a soft latino rock,
Sharpy would dim the lounge lights
and we'd lay on the lush carpet
full of Lambrusco and unspecified potentials.
Sunday morning we'd slope off down to 'The Village'
to watch the lined old men at chess outside Panucci's
and I'd wonder how it would all play out.

Thou Art

We embraced Rauschenberg's goat, its shaggy expressionism,
a long-haired sofa strafed by a hagiography of paint bullets
and household waste. We had gone for the big peruse
all the long way from Primitivism to Stella
back to MoMA, on to the power house of modern art
where Elvis Presley as Kid Kiowa stroked

his six-gun from its holster, twice over, a stroke
of genius in the hair department, the liquid empiricism
of quiff, sidearm and bandanna – Pop-art's
sharpshooter and soft-core Billy
the Kid. 'What's Elvis' middle name?' you asked. 'Costello?'
I said, not without a certain persiflage,

as you might say. Then and thence did we ever pootle,
all agog, from Guggenheim to El Prado to St Rocca,
stroll beneath our *noche enstrellado*,
as it would appear in our lover's encomium.
You were my Yankee kid bride to be, baby,
before the world we made went pop! Art

thou a maid, Elvira Madigan? Thou art
more lovely and yet the pursuit
of happiness vouchsafed by the bullet
leaves something to be desired. The stroke

of dawn remembers me looking at you, kid: an Etruscan
village and you at the embers, my *Cenorentola*,

a single burst of lightning to the cerebellum
or the vibrations of *il preludio* of the heart,
you were giving me excitations,
but we twain paramours *paresseux*
could never kid ourselves it would all be OK'd
by a tall stranger in a white hat. *Perhaps this silver bullet . . . ?*

The Bronx, the Brooklyn Bridge, the Bowery,
the Big A, where the face of Marilyn doubles for the face of Drella
living *la vie Americaine*. The stroke
of midnight and the graffiti kid dangles over the El, spraying art
on the bridges across from the loft studios of Parnassus,
where yous and Is implement their breathy existentialisms:

the expression of the *danse macabre* or *ballet
amoureux*. 'Lovers do nothing on purpose, kid,' whispers Ella,
and what comes of that, as in art, is by that one stroke.

Composed on the Millennium Bridge on the Morning of its Re-opening 22nd February 2002

City of random architectures, effluvia and bridge
in which we debouch onto the new Millennium:
Plexiglas, hawser and the old marriage
of the here and now to the wide world's conundrum.
I study the high-boned colourings of your face,
hot medallions in a cold circumstance;
my words scream out in the torque and race
of wind, *'scape this temporal 'cumbrance*,
or whatever. My God, what is is neither fair
nor foul nor favourable, I say, before the spot where
you ask, 'Why leave for a thing you already have?'
Circumspice and the blue, blue neon on the blue air
tops out the buildings, fashionably, there to here.
I say, 'Because', then 'the way over is the way back.'

Bricolage

Il existe une histoire de la Ste Jeanne d'Arc,
quelque part dans les bibliothèques, sur les rayons obscurs,
des textes perdus que personne n'connaît,
quelque part où même un rat de bibliothèque
ne fouillerait point, tout au fond
graves à l'eau forte en noir—noir, noir, noir.
Dans ce conte la sainte sanglotte,
le sol tremble comme les mains d'un dipso
et toutes les chandelles dansantes s'éteignent.

Tu dois le savoir parce que tu l'ais vu de tes propres yeux
quand tu me regardes lorsque tu dis que moi,
je pourrais être maréchale des armées,
une soldate moderne et féroce. Et je pleure,
je pleure assez pour éteindre un incendie de forêt
et dis que si je l'étais, je te brûlerais la cervelle.

Reproduced here is a version, in French, of my poem *Breakages*. It was written and sent to me by the French poet Solange Devagine. Her English prose translation is as follows:

'There exists a report of Joan of Arc somewhere in the libraries, the dark shelves, the unknown lost texts, somewhere even a real bookworm would not look, right at the back, etched in black. In this account the Saint breaks into sobs, the earth trembles like the hands of a drunkard and all the candles that dance extinguish themselves. You should know this because you have seen it with your own eyes when you regard me when you say that I, I could be a field marshal, a ferocious, contemporary woman soldier and I weep, I weep enough to put out a forest fire and say that if I were I would blow your brains out.'

Out to Lunch Poem

I sit amidst the mandrills in the coffee bar and grill.
The waitress has seen me inside-out already:
I wear my oesophagus as a tie and gulp all the way down
to my duodenum; I am an organogram, a biology lesson.
Why did I ever hide my inner self?
I will display me, will be intestines off the shelf.
One eye and two mouths is the arrangement
I've come to with my face;
it concentrates the vision, but binocularises taste.
I lick the tabletop – it tastes of surface
and half-past one in the afternoon.

The 'drills put down their power lunch
and howl amongst themselves at some joke.
The alpha-male makes a call on his cellphone,
barks *Jesus Christ! where is he?*
His nose burns blue with the conversation,
his backside flashes an insane traffic light that can't quite decide
whether to stop, go, or maybe.

I am here, my child, as new as the world and as old as a baby.
I've spent a century inspecting the fractal squared design
of the actual linoleum, it spills into a chess board
with the me as the Messiah king, the waitress

as Mary Magdalen and the pawns miniature mandrills
wearing sandals and the faces of the apostles.

I cross the waitress with my benediction of paper money
and easy coinage, return to where I am, always have been
and will be forever and ever. Ahem.

Why

Above you like a horse, my nostrils fire heat
on the maroon disruption of duvet and bedlinen;
the artery in my neck slams blood up my head.
A voided gin bottle, its final smear in your tumbler,
informs your blowsy mouth with its juniper come-ons.
Veronica, the sparkling of my *Aqua Pura* is the sadder noise –
those *pétillant* increments,
the frowns of angels on their pinheads calling:
Beware, beware she dyes her hair – her eyes are green.

I extend my shadow across you;
the bedclothes murmur like rumours.
I put it all down to your henna'y reveal,
your eyes sharp as limes.
Your question undoes me to myself,
offers what I want to have you want me to.

The Varieties of Impression: Sunrise, Massachusetts

You can see the Boeings in their brutal insouciance
to the laws of nature rise up out of Logan bound for God.
The sensational lake of the bay deflects the sun's cool explosion
and the blue-green freedom of the seawaters
gives fresh evidence for everything.
But Independence Day hasn't come round yet
and the underswells and currents present
as a moment of enormous trouble
like a passenger jet off-flightpath headed for daytime TV.

You can't fall into the same sea twice,
as Icarus found when his fangly wings
dripped him like a drop of candle wax
into the Aegean with a hiss
and all his dad's super-adhesive technologies
couldn't tape him back up again. The poor booby,
just looking for a real hot tan
before the idiom of the sun-ray lamp.

The eyes of the young men fishing with their sail-boats
and new accessory coolboxes
gloss the water. A white gull takes the air,
the pale sun of its sternum ignites
the turning bronze weathervane of a sea bass.
A mockingbird rehearses its appropriated melodies,

a thousand throats in one, never settling;
it is a thing to know the heart's desire,
who one is in the voice of another.
The eddies seem to suspend for a moment;
the gull turns an eye,
and the clock of the Yacht Club stops
corroding for an instant.

Deep inside everything is a memory.
I once saw the glaze of a live fish sliced into,
they excised its heart,
but it continued to beat on a dish
driving itself on and onwards and on –
the sockeye return to their shallows and mountain pools,
and even the cool shoreline rocks conceal
what sustains them.

You can't fall into the same *anything* twice,
not life, nor a summer with a thousand Julys,
now drank, now dry.
                    So we wait
for the approaching holiday
with the flags ready on their sad white spindles,
each star a hand print.
Do it for all of us, they are saying.

The latest flights inscribe their meticulous azimuths
a mile above Misery Island, the rock, the hard place,
where the human dream has faltered
through the ascent of mankind
all the way from Hiawatha to Gary Cooper.
You can wreck yourself calling out there –
those delicate rapprochements, these *petits baisers*.
But no island is a man.

Then from afar I hear ancestral voices prophesying eggs,
coffee, OJ and the News that *is* News.
The seagull lands; the bass dive away;
the fishermen bide their time;
as the Atlantic waters beat against their own undertow,
as waters do, as waters do,
and it's coming on Independence Day.

The Marshes

for LH

Solitary men walk as if with a purpose, hands grown
down into their pockets. The sacred birds
send up their flights alone
into the air. Each one calls its absurd
course of notes, each arpeggio
every scrambled call for its mate
or object of desire to decode.
The bravado illustrates
the blank air – the skylark engraves the sky
with the Spirograph of its release:
the tumbling spirit it finds itself. The hours
absorb the men, they tramp beneath the cry
of the birds, observe them, or else
look for their souls among the marsh flowers.

Flower Market Street

The air today is so brilliant you have to breathe it in sunglasses,
the clouds in their short-sleeved cotton shirts
as fresh as the people of Rome
who make their way back to work
after their siesta and shower and who look
like someone has starched and ironed them
and as if something has been *arranged*.

And perhaps it would have been better, *padre mio*,
have avoided all that trouble, if you'd stayed there,
learned to really speak the lingo, hadn't had to mangle
those Caruso songs on Sunday mornings,
married the one wife, her eyes like olives.

Instead you practised the ancient drill:
the blinds lowered in daylight,
the fatuous fables of where you've been,
all the flimsy ad hoc'ery of deceit.
You knew the preposterous offset of weekday afternoons
that were your Saturday nights,
the new cufflinks you dared not use,
the birthday cakes you only had one slice of, the whole catastrophe
of stolen temporalities from the gaps of your life.

A certain woman and I stroll your neighbourhood
and she remarks how fitting it is
that she should be the one here with me –
not being who we are, being who we are not –
as we walk your street out of time.
'It seems,' I tell her, 'I have a gift for all this.'

We pass the bedroom window of your mid-life,
the boudoir, the love-nest.
This was the fling that sent you off your own fancy way
in your Italian suits and *Agua de Silva* –
my shining one, with your daring blend of deception and romance.
I stand here now, stand here then,
as once again you steal out
to come home to kiss goodbye to my childhood.
I say, *Go to it, don't let me down,*
that I might come to write you this;
and you didn't.

Ask Them

Ask them all where it is hid;
ask the old man and the kid,
fortune tellers in their stripy tents,
circus artists, governments,
cyclists round the velodromes,
Rosicrucians, garden gnomes.
Enquire politely of city women in their fashion heels;
ask the sturgeons, lampreys and the conger eels.
Go to Lourdes, Delphi, London Zoo;
lobby wolverine and kangaroo.
Humbly petition the Arapaho
(if it were known, surely they would know).
Look in each house, each studio flat;
pray to God from Mt Ararat.
Ask them, ask them every one;
examine the poles, go to the sun.
You will not find a single clue;
it is no longer there for you.

A Younger Woman

The long huts hunched above the Arctic circle.
The slow veil of sunshine failed and failed
onto the solid earth. In this un-place
insects froze to a halt and dropped from the air
as individual sleet; hail ball-bearings fired
onto the marble ground with a crack yet leaving no crack;
icicles pierced sheet steel when they fell.
                              A single stove per hut
around which, nightly, the zeks would lie in a decaying spiral
like the orbit of a Soviet space hulk.
Daybreak, they would haul out the lumpen bundles
of those next to the stove, their thin ghosts
unable to hold onto the dear bodies they had played in
in kindergarten under gentler protocols.
Night on night, the men would cleave themselves a row nearer,
drawn by the trace-memory of that warmth,
                              fleeting and indelible,
knowing that when they held it full and close
it would let them go but once.